sort/quantum

Mark Cunningham

sort/quantum

© 2023 by Mark Cunningham

All rights reserved.

Published by Mark Cunningham

ISBN 979-8-218-16853-7

Thanks to Linda Kobert, Christopher Simmons, harry k stammer, Amy Stephenson, and Mark Young.

Earlier versions of some of these pieces have appeared in *BlazeVox, Country Music, decomP, Defenestration, The Destroyer, e.ratio, Everyday Genius, Futures Trading, kill author, Kugelmas, Möbius, Molly Bloom, Otoliths, Queen Mob's Tea House, Really System, Right Hand Pointing, Six Sentences, Streetcake, Unlikely Stories, Zombie Logic Review*, and the chapbook *X-ray Glasses* (NAP).

sort/quantum

sort

Franz Kline magnified a detail of one of his drawings and discovered another Franz Kline. She wrote herself a note to remind herself to write a note next time. Another mathematician with a boutique infinity. A player piano can play more notes at one time than two human hands as long as the power stays on, so you can get bored quicker and stay bored longer. I said I always make a bad first impression, and he pointed out that every moment is happening for the first and only time.

My idea to make people with jazz hands into semaphore flaggers didn't work out so well; then I proposed that they work airport security, and that's going great. She winked (signal) and he thought she had a tick (noise). He winked (signal) and she got the message (noise). Our candidate wanted to have a debate on the issues, but theirs didn't, so we got into an argument about that. The committee voted to train mockingbirds instead of hiring more therapists: after all, the birds can repeat a statement back in the speaker's own way of speaking or change their language to present a new view.

I didn't recognize him until somebody told me he was famous. We're cooler than they are, because it's the spaces between our ". . ." rather than the dots that are important. He realized he was in a stare-down match with his blind spot, so he was defeated before he even got started. She said she was sensitive to her environment: it was good sleeping weather. An Alzheimer's pill? I can't even remember to take my vitamin.

The hair on your arms forms patterns that are A) you or B) not you. The committee told him it didn't count if he gave himself the nickname. I keep confusing mean and median, so I must be average after all. Identity Crisis Doesn't Change Who You Are. Usually only other people can see the image on your retina.

Somebody named Midge *sounds* likeable, but it turns out I didn't *like* like her—pretty weak hypnosis. We stood in the field by a sign that read LAND with an arrow pointing off to the left. We knew we were the bad guys when we ran out of ammunition first. Now I feel cheap: my inferiority complex isn't as paralyzing as any of theirs. "You know what I mean" is always a good phrase to use in a rock song.

It's hard to say how much you'd get out of a book titled *How to Read a Book* unless you already knew how to read a book. Stepping back from the telescope, she said she couldn't tell if she was seeing the darkness of infinite space, or just the dust blocking the view of the darkness of infinite space. The abstract painting was amazing: no matter where we stood, it looked out of focus. He told me not even to think about destroying the world, so I opened another franchise location and didn't think about it.

He claimed the new material was "many fold as abundant" as the old, but we noticed it kept getting smaller. "We used to talk. Only all he'd say was words." In her email, she threatened to go postal, so we figured she was already running out of steam.

We asked management for a clearer definition of "such matters as the origin of the world," and the representative stalled for a few days, and even when he told us we could tell he was just making stuff up. After the storage pond evaporated, the tech people said they still had the water, only now it was stored in the cloud. Is Mindfulness Just Another Fad, or Is It a Life-Changing Skill? He pointed out that even inside a cave, you can see the horizon, since the horizon is the limit of your seeing.

The filmmaker said, "It's impossible to be 24-hours-a-day real." Once analysis showed that the grounds of the natives' existence were decaf, we figured we'd have them pacified in no time. We vowed to throw in the towel and stop polluting the reservoir, but the towels we'd already thrown in had absorbed all the water. The apartment was only back-projected, so the rent was low enough I could afford it. Seeing is believing, but what she believes most is that she blinks.

Last night, I looked out the window and it was so dark I couldn't see a thing; this morning, I have a vivid memory of not seeing a thing. When he didn't do well on the test, he pointed out the pupils of your eyes are black because the light that enters *never returns*. I always like the guy who, in a forty-second-long film from 1903, say, stands at edge of Niagara Falls and points to the rushing water, so you'll know what to look at. They proved I didn't exist—as if I was going to let something like that crimp my self-confidence.

After she caught her breath, she said it's when people are choking like that and can't speak that they need help, and I said now you tell me. His essay "The Writing of *The Writing of Disaster*" turned out to be a real mess. I thought they were laughing *with* me, but then I remembered Buckminster Fuller's definition of the universe as a system of non-simultaneous events. We raised our right hands and repeated the pledge, "I will be true to myself, in so far as in me lies." He said he had a feeling all this had happened before, and she said, "What else is new?"

When the doctor told me I was so out of shape I was almost a blob, I wasn't sure if I should concentrate on my diet and exercise more or just relax and let gravity do its work, and then I remembered that gravity's work *is* to concentrate. We made sure the rayon shrunk as soon as it was washed: that way, it looked like we didn't use so many trees to make it. If there are only a few tears, they taste salty and delicious on French fries.

When he said the river was polluted and the eco-system out of balance, she pointed out that gray goes with everything. So what if there are only a few twigs left of the rain forest: now it matches the rest of our IKEA stuff. The mountain had been so mined out that the boulders were made of Styrofoam, so getting caught in the avalanche didn't hurt that much. We changed the definition of noise pollution from "uproar" to "uproarious," and now everybody is happier.

Nobody showed up for the premiere of his play *Performing Privacy*, so he changed the title to *Preforming Privacy* and had a hit. She said the term *Selbstetzungslehre* meant *self-positioning subject*, and we said we'd take her word for it. I hope he's right when he says the treatment "dissipates tumors beyond belief," because I don't believe him. At least I was the "this" in their list of "this, that, and the other thing." Still optimistic: broken *up*.

Now that my hairspray has helped destroy the ozone layer, I have to use even more of it to protect against the solar wind. Something about the Paul Celan Fan Club didn't sound right, but after we changed the title of Pierre Joris's translation from *Lightduress* to *Liteduress*, Singles Nite really took off, so I just went with it.

We shared a moment, but she still got the half with the most cranberries. I said, "You know how good friends can just sit and say nothing," and he said, "Shut up." The second person stacked the bricks that had been laid end-to-end, but only the first person was called a genius. We swept the dust and dirt into a plastic bag and took it to the landfill. When he said don't believe every voice you hear in your head, I knew right away which one I'd start with.

I threw the car air freshener out the window, but it's okay—the cardboard was cut in the shape of a pine tree. We kept underexposing the photograph until finally it was a work of art. They call it the "vanishing point," but it never really goes away. So I didn't save the day: at least I invented Daylight Saving Time.

The guy at the gas station gave us directions to the Lost Highway. "Concerning the Alpine Larch the fact which even most naturalists know best is that they have never seen it." Scratching his beard, the old-timer said he remembered the Indian braves dancing at Disneyland. When she heard the phase "ghost rain," her mouth began to water.

They wanted to call our air freshener "Cool Breeze," but I convinced them to call it "Mountain Fresh," so we could charge more. She said all places were the same, and I said where did you get that idea? Left onto the sidewalk, right at the corner, two blocks straight, another right into the parking lot: the Slurpee Trail. Tears are so natural, they have to be lit just right. "Aftermath is the new national parks scenery." He said he *was* paying attention: it was the continent that was drifting.

An environmentalist waits until the third beer before he throws the empty bottle into the woods. No one says the moon is half empty.

Evergreen—for two years. The spokesperson insisted all the death metal t-shirts were made from organic cotton. We named the liquor store after the college team's mascot, so you bet we're concerned about the environment. She was depressed because she couldn't live near the ocean, and then she realized she could make her own spreading patch of junked plastic milk cartoons and soda bottles in the backyard. Many people don't believe the Wright Brother's plane from Kitty Hawk on display at the Smithsonian is the original, because it's too clean.

He's nostalgic for the days of Neo-. When I get anxious about the future, I hold a Styrofoam cup to my ears, and the sound of the surf calms me.

His new asceticism: to make as boring as possible conversation in restaurants or coffee shops. I ran out of wool halfway through my cloned macramé fractal show, so now I'm working on origami paper wads.

Scanning the dunes that went on for miles in every direction, he said, "Here we are, up a creek without a paddle." Suburbanites Live in Diverse Areas. The busy bodies protested our Astroturfing the moon. She said, "We are all individuals," and I thought, who am I to disagree? The other guy from Wham!

The instructions said there's more sense of a gaze if you see the whites of the eyes. Boris Karloff played some of the greatest monsters in film history; off-screen, he was one of the most boring people ever to live. The sign at the restaurant said Now Serving You, so she went somewhere else for lunch. Wow, I'm kind of an anti-essentialist, too.

A *Kodiak* bear, not a Kodak bear—wish I'd heard that right the first time. Choose one: the two main characters in George Romero's *Dawn of the Dead* who die and turn into zombies are A) less creepy or B) more creepy than the extras shuffling around the shopping mall. Earthlight is blue; TV light is blue; therefore, Ryan Seacrest is natural. Dear Michael Jackson: I want to be the first person to moon walk on the moon.

I don't know about being "a pair of ragged claws scuttling across the floors of silent seas," but I like to watch my DVD of jellyfish while I listen to Brian Eno. Dear Oscar Wilde: nature imitates 1970s porn films more than 1970s porn films imitate nature: "thick, fluent tufts." The background: *"Western Hemlocks, Cedars, titanic Douglastrees, and great Lowland Firs come rushing toward you, are passed, fall behind, and then seem to spring reborn out of the horizon ahead."*

He was voted Indian Most Likely to Get His Foot Caught in the Stirrups after He'd Been Shot Out of the Saddle. According to neurologists, it takes about a half second for the "time on" function of the conscious mind to activate after a nerve receives a stimulus (reflex reacts much faster), so everything really is a rerun. The inspector drew a chalk outline to show where the Dover cliffs had been. Yahoo headline, 8 October 2009: NASA Aims at the Moon. We had to invent our own laugh track, so don't say we weren't original.

When they didn't understand the directions for the connect-the-dots, she said, "Do I have to draw you a picture?" Everything can be considered "almost circular in outline" if you finish tracing the outline. Dear Carl Jung: there's a part of the subconscious mind that recognizes every oldie played on the radio within the first five notes. I think of Mount Shasta every time I want a cheap soda.

If I could vomit up every moment of my life so far, I would, but I can't afford another sick day. Trying to understand her lecture "Beyond Energy" left us too exhausted to go to the reception afterwards. The biologist told him he'd need bigger eyes or a bigger brain, but the overhead costs would be more than the budget allowed. I mean that "hmmm" on many levels. He kept saying "praxis" instead of "practice" just to irritate the test chimp. She said no ideas but in Sting.

I thought the guy was making a Black Power salute, but then he pulled off to the right. So what if nobody can remember my name—my high-tech foam cushion remembers the shape of my ass. Now that we've pretty much destroyed the world, we're going to have to advertise the hell out of it to get people to think it's real. Once they moved in and got used to the radiation from the power lines in the back yard, they realized the plate in her head made perfect grilled cheese sandwiches. First bones, then moving pictures and TV shows, and now any thought you happen to think: the evolution of fossils.

Love isn't always on time; he isn't always on time; nevertheless, they do not love him. In *A Hard Day's Night*, John Lennon puts a cola bottle to his nose—sniffing coke—but it's a Pepsi bottle. Using footage of Jimmy Stewart and Kim Novak in our Stairmaster commercial was a natural.

He said it was unpleasant to think about ghosts right after you've masturbated. Taxidermy Gone Hilariously Wrong. When it's turned off, the TV reflects my life *even more*.

He said the object was convex, which located it only in relation to him, and he was lost, so we figured the object was, too. They said, "Whenever we describe the motion of dead objects, this anthropomorphism comes into its own," but all I'd said was, "My nose is running." It wasn't a mirage: they just hadn't taken the plastic wrap off the artificial dust yet. He insisted that looking through the wrong end of a telescope *is* a form of introspection.

Do it yourself fractals: you eat corn on the cob and corn rubble gets stuck between your teeth and when you smile your mouth looks like a cob of corn. Thanks to global warming, I can give her dirty looks and not have to worry about my face freezing like that. We grew up thinking the joke, "I know how to spell 'banana'—*ba-na-na-na-na*—but I don't know when to stop" was hilarious, and now we work in genetic engineering.

Charles Bukowski has had more books published since he died than most writers get out while they're alive. "Pixilated" used to mean you'd drunk too much; now it means you've been absorbed. We had to pick out the American Spirit cigarette butts before they were convinced the ashes were those of their ancestors. "Are pride parades for bank-sponsored floats or actual gay people?" Every time the speaker said "Das Ding!" we started to salivate.

Once a star has burned most of its hydrogen, it starts helium fusion and produces carbon, oxygen, and neon, so no wonder the night sky looks gaudy. She pointed out that silicon made up 13 to 15 percent of the earth's weight, and that meant her figure was totally natural. "Tacky" means I can feel it. He said he regained his sanity by acting like a jerk all the time, which embarrassed his second personality so much it finally stopped showing up.

Particle and/or wave: so that's how the eyelash ends up in my eye. A comb over, like the rest of nature, evolves with barely perceptible slowness, until it seems inevitable. "So many bad teeth. The dolphin will laugh at you." "The sperm cell circles the egg forever, producing nothing," was not the correct answer: it was "NASCAR racing."

They banned our porn film *The Erotic Adventures of a Penny*, because they wanted to take pennies out of circulation. Now that somebody has told the Baptists about Plato and they've noticed how a fire's shifting light makes your shadow move even when you're standing still, they're more against dancing than ever. My declaration of universal love was judged to have harassed everybody. $i + i = -1$. He said it was concave-convex, she said it was convex-concave, so they called the whole ocean off.

She got all psyched up to help with the reforestation project, but then she couldn't find a shady spot. We burned all the maps so no one would find us, and then we remembered the name of our town is Ashland. When he saw how big his ass looked in the Godzilla suit, he felt like a total mutant. I took everything with a grain of salt, and now you're telling me that's why I have high blood pressure? Even as our raft circled nearer the center of the whirlpool, the idea of a sucking void made us laugh.

At the end of the last movie, the monster fell 80,000 feet to certain death, but its nervous system is too slow for the message to have reached its brain yet, so it will act like it's still alive long enough to finish the sequel. I changed the title of my long poem from *The Cantos* to *The Can Tos*. They kept saying the answer was negative seven, and we kept asking, "Are you positive?" He said I was slack jawed, but I said my discourse was an "open formation." She proved conclusively that we were moving backwards in time, which left us all pretty depressed, until we realized we wouldn't remember any this when we woke up, and that gave us something to look forward to.

The guru said you can cover the world with leather or make yourself a pair of shoes, so we sprayed the homeless with deodorant until they'd built up a weather-resistant layer of aluminum. She got cancer from her cell phone and insurance wouldn't pay, so she moved closer to one of the towers to get free radiation. A simple genetic jiggle, and people can jog rather than walk in their sleep, and those extra pounds will just melt away. To get good market share, we named our hair product The Human Conditioner. He always types "momento mori" before spell check reminds him it's "memento mori."

When he saw me struggling to breathe, he opened a bag of Doritos for me, because there's always plenty of air in one of those. Now that all of us at the insurance company have become existentialists, we've decided that every surgery is elective. Cure Arthritis with a Raisin. I became suspicious when my new liver squeaked and dogs tried to jump on me every time I bent over, but, hey, it's great to be popular. "Some people live mighty fine lives with inoperable brain tumors." For Halloween, the Infection Control Department decorated its door with cutouts of happy ghosts.

We decided that having the seven-year-old shout, "That guy's walking off with our carcinogens" would jump start the big chase. The line, "Think about your career!" always got a big laugh. She took that pie chart right in the kisser. He's standing closer to the magnetic North Pole, but I can wave my hands higher in the air. If you repeat "Jacques Lacan" over and over, it sounds like you're saying "Chaka Khan."

She branded the campaign Endless Summer, and she made the interns vow never to let up. The spokesperson said, "The job of selling must be done with feeling," and pointed to a chart that listed the stages of the sales process, beginning with "The Approach" and ending with "Closing the Sale," each of which was marked by a shoe print. We were going to build a border wall, but we couldn't find enough illegals to work for the lousy wages, so the whole thing went nowhere. I convinced the farmhands that origins were unrecoverable, all the while stressing that since acquired characteristics are not inheritable, the egg comes first.

One of the earliest stages of the embryo is the blastocyst; therefore, we grow up and like programs with explosions in them. I got interested in environmental protection when I learned some trees were "pistol-butted." She takes nitroglycerin because she's heard that little detonations are good for you. "I am not afraid of dying. I am a really positive person. I can take it."

I assured him that no man is an island, but I think he could tell I was just treading water. She picked herself up by her shoelaces: the Nikes had cut off the circulation to her feet. Shinkichi Takahasi found mountains and rivers inside a single potato; I found a notice reading "Copyright Monsanto." When the clerk told her the oxygen prescription had expired, she threatened to hold her breath until she could talk to a manager. He told the judge that it wasn't so much that he'd stabbed me, as that I'd reified the knife blade.

The air strikes weren't doing much good, so the president sent over one of those giant cookies from the mall, and *that* put the bastards out of action. Turns out the shepherd hadn't been rabid: we'd been fooled by his milk mustache.

"All truth has to be expressed in sentences because all truth is *the transference of power*. The type of sentence in nature is a flash of lightning." The commercial for "Values" featured Louis Armstrong singing "It's a Wonderful World" while computer-generated lightning broke over mountains. You a) would or b) would not cross a bridge built by an engineering firm named Suspension of Disbelief.

Dear Seneca: we, too, have learned that "when a few bodies move about in a great open space, they are not able to ram into each other, or to be pushed around," so we defunded Planned Parenthood and increased the military budget. The essay was titled "How Antlers Help Pro Athletes," but we thought that seemed pretty obvious. After she saw the book *Animals Without Backbones*, she stopped donating to the Sierra Club. Now that I'm into death metal, I consider my nipples umlauts.

Researchers: Being Bad at Relationships is Good for Survival. Company Turns Loved One's Ashes into Hunting Ammo.

She kept trying to tell her joke, but they kept hitting her just as she got to the punch line. He said, "change is inseparable from the account of it," and I was ready to continue the conversation when I noticed him turn his hearing aid off. I hope I never hear the phase "This isn't your aunt's Renaissance Fair," but I heard it in my head when I wrote it. Of course it all went up in smoke: that's how you make smoke signals.

He went on digital high-def television to state that poets are still the antennae of the race. "A continual hint of the philosophical relevance of the impossibility of content"—or words to that effect. The police officer had a different view of "uncorrected proof" than I did. We had them all excited about a book titled *Reincarnation Now!* but then a rerun of *The Golden Girls* came on and distracted them. The blurb writers spent so much time being "astonished" and "stunned" that finally we just let them become totally unconscious.

I said our corporation was no longer a driving force in society, and he said we were located in an industrial park for a reason. The ideogram means "Man Standing By His Word," or so the committee decided after checking the dictionary. We told them they didn't have to worry about our leaving a carbon footprint, because we weren't leaving. My sense of guilt pushes me toward suicide, but there comes a time when you just have to stop the violence.

We got together to discuss our report on individuality, and I said whatever he wanted to do was fine with me and he said whatever I wanted to do was fine with him, so we got nothing done. I asked in what way was I lacking, and he said he'd run out of words before he finished, so I figured we were equal.

I said her left hand looked smaller than her right hand, but she said it was just a sleight of hand. Our model is for educational purposes, so it's OK if it's shoddy. The study found that the central nervous system is an exception. He said, "everything is the result of contingent perception and the 'truth' is an invention," and when we seemed skeptical, he said, "I'm *not* making this up." They said they didn't care if it's spelled "telephony," it's still a science.

Elephant Seal Really Wants a Kiss. Utah Boy Sets Record By Keeping 43 Snails On Face. "When a costumed deer does a backflip from a ladder 10-feet above the rim, you've got to show him some love." She told us to tell the animals we wouldn't be suffering from delusion anymore. Astronauts Finish Work on Hubble, Give It Goodbye Hug.

After we explained how the universe is a constant flux of ricocheting vibrations, it was easy to get the military to hand over $735 for a screwdriver. Not so much that she's a pluralist, as that she makes subject-verb agreement errors. His second personality had a schizophrenic episode, and he lasted all its life. According to the map, every place is an outskirt. I close my eyes: I still see. I sleep: my eyes still move.

All other options exhausted, we made black the new black. "But that's the universe," he said in a dubbed voice, and lowered the visor of his space helmet.

quantum

They led her in a circle and called it a revolution. "DNA has a real attraction to alcohol." She told me to suspect all beginnings, and I said, "When do I start?" When he complained that the lenses of our X-ray glasses were so dark he couldn't see through *them*, let alone anybody's clothes, we told him we'd given him the new, improved set, and he was seeing through time as well as space—all the way back to before the Big Bang!

When he said the Comfy Recliner Chair Time Machine wasn't working, the tech assistant explained that since it was a budge model it didn't have the speed, power, or range of the more expensive ones, but if he sat there and had patience, he'd get to the future. We blurred the photograph until people couldn't figure out what was going on: that way, they'd know something was going on. Well, it was *more* experience, mathematically speaking. Nightmares burn calories faster.

The light indexed in a photograph is still moving, since you see it. They told me the "right here, right now" line formed over there.

I said it was my "big day," but they said that, after a certain age, people start to shrink. Though nothing happened for a whole year, the physicist proved our bodies continue to give out personal information. The News anchor gave good plausible denial, but her dentistry was totally unbelievable. He said she was fast forwarding her shadow at him in a subliminal fill-in-the-blank; she said she was materializing the trace of her delay.

"Here are the test results. It contains only calcium." "What percentage?" "Ninety percent." Standing naked out in the middle of the woods, I couldn't remember a poem, only the assurance that, "when everything else has been taken from you, a memorized poem remains." His middle initial stood for no name.

That "my" arm has gone numb is just an idea. I didn't understand about 10% of his "give 110%" speech, but after he curved the grades I did fine. She said, "I think I've lost my credibility," but I said, "Don't you believe it." He walked into the room totally naked, and the panel said, "Get real." She's a ghost all right, but we can't decide if that makes her a minimalist or maximalist of being.

You can't step into the same river twice—unless it's been syndicated. The sky is a blue screen. *Arrival* was listed as the third of the three phases of displacement. The traumatic event never happened, but people still fall ill from breathing the radon seeping through the foundations of the therapist's office.

When I said, "At night, everybody has a black eye," she punched me. He said, "Depth leads to projection," but I didn't understand that, so I figured he was just another idiot. We voted to "oppose the formation of a new cliché that would make us sink lower than low." No point having five copies if you're going to keep them all in the same place—this statement used to refer only to inanimate objects. She wanted to clarify whether they said they'd see her *inside* or see her *insides*.

The band is so authentic, it can be repackaged in many different ways. They said that wasn't my identity; it was only my "identity position." The role of Antonin Artaud was played by Conrad Veidt for all of Artaud's life. I can never complete the connect-the-dot erotic drawing so the figures come out normal, so I must be tantric. My big break came when my arm was cast as itself.

The instructions said to ignore the fact that the picture of the object was another object. A fleck of dead skin, a floater, stops being part of my eye and becomes part of the visible world. The taste in my mouth is the taste of my mouth.

Since form is never more than extension of content, I did a tap dance and sang, "Why don't we drink a couple of beers and have a tacky time?" but Samantha wasn't impressed. We could tell Fred was upset about the committee's saying he wouldn't look cutest on the milk carton. Just because I ate some of Jim's French fries when he wasn't paying attention does *not* mean I identify too much with other people's desires. We assured them we were laughing *with*, not *at*, their laugh track. Next time, make the moment special: write a note using a glitter pen.

They told her that her ultrasound had been made before she was born, but she said she still had things to say. Sound travels farther under water, so no matter where they are we can make the blue whales listen to *America's Got Talent*.

The directional redistribution of waves of light for specific results, such as the induction of glare = solar polarization. That was to over-stated clichés what Michelangelo was to painting. Due to inflation, the honor of being Miss Universe 2010 covers a larger area and is less an honor than being Miss Universe 1959. The magazine praised him for working "like some relentless human-rights robot."

After he confused navy blue for black yet again, he got a notice stating that he'd been demoted from "himself" to "hisself." Now that the neighbors have replaced their windows with reflecting glass, I've become only a narcissist.

They had the Word That Must Not Be Spoken; we had the word that no one could figure out how to pronounce. When he said he was going to make some sweeping changes, we asked him to make a commercial when he was done so we'd know. I am my own worst enemy, and I will overcome this problem through self-reliance: interesting things happen if you get depressed enough. The first thing the lab ape drew with the pencils we gave it was the bars of its cage, which struck us all as pathetic, so we made it some eyeglasses.

As soon as she put the seashell to her ear, she knew the ocean wasn't digital. You can tell your age by how many fast food chains you remember that are no longer in business. From Pompeii to cinder blocks: the trickle-down theory of civilization. He keeps waiting for his Performance underwear to *do* something. A recurring dream: they're pinching me.

But my hair style goes so well with fast food visors. He said, "Most of us have had some experience of childhood." They told her that she was anthropomorphizing the neighbors. The booklet asked, "If you were a shape, what shape would you be?" and he wondered what the author thought would be reading this. The teenager said a mutant race of violent mole people was rising from the sewers, but we didn't believe him, since such prejudice could come only from ignorance.

The doctor looked at the shadow of my hand and said it was a dog. There wasn't a listing for *Index* in the Index.

She said I looked taller in the photograph, which made me feel self-conscious, since in the photograph I was only two inches tall. Turns out the 80-foot-long boar-alligator thing wasn't back-projected—we were. Heck, I remember when everybody thought it was some kind of weird mistake when one of your fillings started to broadcast a radio commercial.

The advertising department fixed the image so that after the two faces looking at each other in profile turned into a vase, the vase couldn't be turned back into two profiles. I thought I was going blind—everything looked grainy and scratchy—but the doctor told me it was just stock footage. The announcer's comment that the team was wasting precious seconds was meant as a compliment. We fooled him: it wasn't a virtual fake, but a real one.

Light might be "the great organizer," but things keep getting in its way. We were going to call our new cartoon character Hegemony Cricket, but Disney put an end to that. My rock garden petrified. I told her I was never sure if she was kidding, and she said you must be joking. When the interrogators asked if she thought speech was what separates humans from animals, she knew better than to say anything. Those antibiotics didn't save the cow, either.

The sun is my quality space and if you know what's good for your health you won't even look at it. Our troops *are* practicing nonviolence; they just aren't very good at it yet. Tarantulas Help Scientists Track How Humans Respond to Fear. She was considerate enough to ask those of us who objected to visibility to raise a hand.

Shooting stars don't usually hit anything: the universe, what a loser. The author switched to the first person only to indicate things he couldn't do. 1,987,614, not 1,987,592: if you're going to be obsessive about the number of germs on the toilet seat, you might as well be accurate. Using technology far beyond human comprehension, the aliens traveled eighty gazillion miles and then didn't see me standing behind a bush. I said I missed my prime because I sneezed right then.

We didn't personify the rocks, because they were too stupid. Magnetic Portals Connect Earth to Sun—no wonder I can't get Mr. Fuzzy's beard on straight. Going boldly: the space shuttle Endeavor "passed through many economically downtrodden areas of Los Angeles during its trek." She had an idea and a light bulb came on over her head, but it was fluorescent and the glare and humming gave her a headache. We explained the earthquake by noting that, after a while, duct tape turns brittle and pieces can chip off.

A lot of rocks and a steep slope, but bouncing always looks festive. You can be illiterate and still get a paper cut. We made it to the moon using the physics of someone who'd just been hit on the head by an apple. The dislocated shoulder he got when she punched him nonetheless gave him a fixed point with which to relativize space.

Further research in DNA: the splat of bird shit on the windshield looks like a dinosaur. The scientific underpinnings of humanism are so out of date that if you still believe in them you aren't fully human. After another Bat-Boy-on-the-cover-of-a-tabloid foul up, we decided to genetically engineer some better genetic engineers. No ego, but a big head: I took steroids to write that sentence. The semi-pro players couldn't spit right.

The corn cob holders looked like little cobs of corn. I was suspicious of tampering: the new plastic didn't come wrapped in plastic. Charlie Brown doesn't have a belly button. She pointed out that "know" and "no" are pronounced the same.

The box for the TV dinner didn't have "As Advertised on TV" on it, so no way was that Salisbury steak going to be good. Food's Latest Embarrassment. School Cafeterias Turn to Psychology in New Approach. So the alien girls plan to eat the boys' brains after feeding them a bunch of donuts? We'll wait until the sugar crash, and then get them. Legs are actually made of food! Embarrassing Terror Bulletin.

Meet a Really Hungry Hamster. The label said the pineapple was size 6. Scientists Find Bigger-Bellied Marmot. Whale Caught on Tape Stealing from Fishing Lines. Killer Whales Fight Instincts to Storm Beaches for Food. The physicists are worried, since under the increased G-Force of blast off, the astronaut's body weight will increase "until he blacks out and loses consciousness." Star May Be Heaviest on Record.

The term used to be "white trash." Now it's "undyed recyclables." "Like flies around a dead deer's asshole," was judged to be a bit *too* colorful a way of expressing our interest. Eating Dirt Could Actually Be Good for Babies. Hume disproved the actuality of cause-and-effect relationships, so there's no real way of knowing how this stain got on my shirt. She was voted most likely to end up as a Bellmer doll. Cotton candy, my foot: I know fiberglass when I taste it.

He's a native American (Utah), and his children go to an under-funded school; I'm a native American (Illinois), and I have a dream catcher; she's a native American (North Carolina), and she lives near a river that's been polluted by industrial dumping. The chairperson said, "Pale face speak with forkéd tongue," and I said I don't care, I still like Michael Jackson.

Origins are unrecoverable, but discounts for day-old donuts had to start sometime. The historian traced her ancestry back to the War of the Roses through the *Beverly Hillbillies*. The Supreme Court ruled the suspect had to tell the police he wished to remain silent. "Everything has to be reinvented, including the morning"— the hold-up is we can't figure out when the new billing day begins. Most of us have never been back to the room where we were born. What origins: Sal Mineo is a good Cheyenne warrior.

The touchstone was displayed behind that museum glass you can stand in front of and cast no reflection, if the lighting is right. "A relation of mystical identity due either to contamination or to an actual spiritual identity." Nobody said anything, but the subtitle read, "Darling!" The Ghost Dance turned out to be the twist, which spooked us all.

He said his love song was about the kind of love song he'd write if he were going to write a love song. Anna O. could recall 108 instances, often including dates, of people walking into a room without her hearing them. All the Easter bunnies I've ever eaten are preserved in my subconscious mind. He called it a singularity, but I still had a feeling of *déjà vu*.

Mackenzie is one of those names that can be either a first or a last name. The envelope contained our second final notice.

It's that time of the week: he's changed his blah-blah from "Have a good weekend?" to "Got any plans for the weekend?" They said it was as obvious as night follows day, but everybody knows that day follows night. Either option would be open to her, so she'd always feel that she'd made a mistake. She told me to keep my dumb ideas to myself, but I said that wasn't dialectical enough. Wait—according to our calculations, this is supposed to be a non-Gwen Stefani year.

She was having a dialogue with absence, and she couldn't get a word in. The taxidermist fixed the wolverine so it still looked intense. They accused me of trying to internalize my blood. What makes a house a home is that you're foreclosed and forced to move out.

He likes to read concrete poetry by the cement pond. Kansas City is mostly in Missouri. "Finishing No. 1 in the country means the world to us." County Building Plan Takes Space to a New Level.

The committee said its new project was "paving the way" back to nature. From the air, the pattern of lights and grids looked like a suburb, but when we tried to land, it turned out to be a fractal. A map presents its readers with between one hundred and two hundred million bits of information, which will be helpful when we remember where we parked the car. He wanted to run the formula to determine the degree of entropy in the universe, but it was late, and we all fell asleep before the computer finished.

We knew something was wrong when we reached the horizon and it crumpled the car's bumper. Since our MP3 player didn't work if you moved while trying to use it, we marketed it as "The Speed of Sound." Due to budget cuts, it was only a part-time eternity. Karl Marx, *Wage Labor and Capital*, Collector's Edition.

The ad said there are 29 dimensions of compatibility; since I live in only 4 dimensions, I can guess how my blind date with Sherry's friend is going to go. Despite believing that, "The moment you love, you are unlimited," she still thinks she looks best in outfits from The Limited. The rental group concluded it didn't know about space, but the number of potential boundaries was infinite. Henri Bergson's 1913 lecture at Columbia University on the vital force of life caused one of New York City's first traffic jams.

My performance piece focused on the "mundane" to increase understanding and tolerance by making the audience realize on a visceral level what we all share in common, so I stood around breathing until everyone got irritated and brought it to an early end. She said she had been "placed in space from an early age," though she didn't say where she'd been before that. They tried to tell him it was his reflection, but ha! he knew it was only a *de*flection of light. After checking the guidelines, it turned out I had the blank page in upside down. Our porn magazine *Airbrushed Two-Dimensionality* sold even better as a PDF.

One's "birth and death, objects of belief, eluding immediate consciousness." The film was about a day in the life of an average 9-year-old, so the board made sure it got an R rating. You'd be upset, too, if the medical center sent you a calendar and it went only to October.

When I said I had two obsessions, she told me to get back in touch when I was ready for serious commitment. Ten years of drought or not, we still had to pay a company to design the sand traps. The test to check his creativity involved copying a drawing of a parrot wearing a pirate's hat. Turns out the billboard slogan *Your life. Your style. Your way.* was for a funeral home.

The most amazing power of Dracula in Tod Browning's film is his ability to pass through that huge spider web covering an entire staircase without getting any strands caught in his hair. When you know it's the last time, the time before becomes the real "last time."

She said, "You have never been more attractive than you are now," though, of course, it took a few microseconds for the sound to reach him. Even in the photographs taken with the telescopic lens, she had "far away eyes." He said, "The movement itself is the only truth," and that stopped us in our tracks. I always fall short of the future by one breath.

If I could control all aspects of my life, I'd stop seeing books telling me how I can take control of all aspects of my life. She felt worn to only a shadow of herself, and then she got a letter saying someone had bought her image rights. He said that since fabrics retain DNA indefinitely, we could chill out about that "dust to dust" stuff. They gave the new organism a name from a dead language, so everybody would understand.

The chairperson reminded us that even a vacuum is a gestalt. The couple stood merely feet away from history.

I asked why she wasn't phenomenal anymore, and she said things happen. The blurb said the book explains what it means to be human, but I've read the whole thing twice, and I still don't understand. We put Dr. Edwards in the box and lowered the lid, realizing it was only when we lifted the lid that the quantum event would take place, and either he would accept the findings of post-Einsteinian physics, or we'd have to close the lid again. Dear Hegel: uh, never mind.

Change: the service rep said the Philly Steak and Cheese was made strictly with chicken to give the customer more variety. Change: he said he doesn't like it when he's just sitting there and a vein on the back of his hand shifts position. Sorry to interrupt, but can you help me find the Discovery Channel again? Change: McDonald's says her day starts at $1.

It's so quiet in space, the satellites can hear a pin number drop. While she sat around doing nothing, the photographs developed. His multicellular phone took us all by surprise.

"When confronted with real time, with the real mysteries of time, there's a kind of central nervous spasm that takes place . . . which just amounts to a sort of all-consuming gag." *Look at any word long enough and you will see it open up into a series of faults, into a terrain of particles each containing its own void.* The mountain gave up its last bit of information so we could understand it, which meant it ceased to exist. She said that woman has the most beautiful voice imaginable, like Gomer Pyle when he stops being Gomer Pyle.

The focus group concluded that we needed to focus more. End-of-Life Advocate Dies.

Also by Mark Cunningham

A Longer Life. Text with video by Dale Wisely. (2022). YouTube. <https://youtu.be/cSWPjndC7fM>.

Future Words. if p then q. (2020)

"f(l)ights." *Otoliths* 56 (Southern Summer 2020). A 110-piece sequence. <www.the-otolith.blogspot.com/2020/01/mark-cunningham.html>.

"Fail Lure." *Otoliths* 52 (Southern Summer 2019). An 81-piece sequence. <www.the-otolith.blogspot.com/2018/11/mark-cunningham.html>.

multizon(e). Text with video by Dale Wisely. Right Hand Pointing. (2019). <www.issues.righthandpointing.net/multizone>.

Alphabetical Basho. Beard of Bees. (2016). <www.beardofbees.com/pubs/Alphabetical_Basho.pdf>.

And Suddenly It's Evening. Beard of Bees. (2014). <www.beardofbees.com/pubs/And_Suddenly_Its_Evening.pdf>.

Regularly Scheduled. Beard of Bees. (2012). <www.beardofbees.com/pubs/Regularly_Scheduled.pdf.>

Scissors and Starfish. Right Hand Pointing. (2012).

Helicotremors. Otoliths. (2012).

specimens. BlazeVOX. (2011).

71 Leaves. BlazeVOX. (2008). <www.blazevox.org/ebk-mCunningham%20REAL.pdf>.

80 Beetles. Otoliths. (2008).

Body Language. Tarpaulin Sky Press. (2008).

www.ingramcontent.com/pod-product-compliance
Lightning Source LLC
Chambersburg PA
CBHW051655040426
42446CB00009B/1145